Copyright © 2024 by Joaquin Velasco

All rights reserved. No part of this publication may be reproduced, distributed, or transmitted in any form or by any means, including photocopying, recording, or other electronic or mechanical methods, without the prior written permission of the author, except in the case of brief quotations embodied in critical reviews and certain other noncommercial uses permitted by copyright law.

This book is a work of non-fiction. Names, characters, businesses, places, events, locales, and incidents are the products of the author's research or used in a factual manner. Any resemblance to actual persons, living or dead, or actual events is purely coincidental.

This edition is published by Kindle Direct Publishing.

Cover Design by: Joaquin Velasco

Book Layout by: Joaquin Velasco

For information regarding permission, email:

intellitexts@email.com

First Edition

Legal Disclosure

The information provided in this book, "Getting Paid - Navigating Real Estate Compensation," is for general informational and educational purposes only. The author, Joaquin Velasco, and the publisher, Intellitexts Publishing, have made every effort to ensure that the information provided herein is accurate and helpful, but they make no representations or warranties of any kind regarding the completeness, accuracy, reliability, suitability, or availability with respect to the content of the book.

The advice and strategies contained herein may not be suitable for every situation. This work is sold with the understanding that the author and publisher are not engaged in rendering legal, accounting, or other professional services. If professional assistance is required, the services of a competent professional should be sought.

Neither the author nor the publisher shall be liable for any loss of profit or any other commercial damages, including but not limited to special, incidental, consequential, or other damages. Readers are advised and need to be aware that the real estate market is dynamic, and regulatory conditions are subject to change. Therefore, readers are encouraged to verify the terms and conditions of real estate transactions and consult with a licensed professional for legal advice pertaining to their particular situation.

This publication is not intended to be used, and should not be used, as a substitute for direct professional advice. While the examples and strategies discussed in the book are based on thorough research and experience, they are presented for illustrative purposes only. Actual real estate markets and financial agreements may vary significantly, and readers should not rely solely on the examples provided in this book for making business decisions.

Any trademarks, service marks, registered trademarks, or registered service marks mentioned in this book are the property of their respective owners and are used for identification purposes only. Such use does not imply endorsement by the trademark owner.

Table of Contents

- Introduction: The Evolution of Real Estate Compensation
    - Overview of changes in real estate compensation models
    - Impact of technological advancements and consumer demands
- Flat Fee Services
    - Understanding Flat Fee Models
    - Setting Your Flat Fee Structure
    - Benefits and Challenges for Agents and Clients
    - Case Studies: Success Stories and Lessons Learned
- Hourly Rates
    - Transitioning to Hourly Billing in Real Estate
    - How to Determine Your Hourly Rate
    - Managing Client Expectations and Billing Transparency
    - Real-Life Applications: When Hourly Rates Work Best
- Fee for Service
    - Breaking Down the Fee for Service Model
    - Itemizing Your Real Estate Services
    - Strategies for Marketing a Menu of Services
    - Client Perspectives: Customizing Their Experience

- Retainer Plus Success Fee
    - The Hybrid Approach: Retainer and Success Fees Explained
    - Calculating Retainers and Success Fees
    - Balancing Upfront Costs with Final Rewards
    - Success Stories: Maximizing Earnings While Providing Value
- Subscription Model
    - Innovating with Real Estate Subscriptions
    - What Services to Include in Your Subscription
    - Building Long-Term Client Relationships Through Subscriptions
- Conclusion
    - Choosing the Right Model for Your Business
    - Adapting to Change and Staying Competitive
    - The Future of Real Estate Compensation
- Appendices
    - Additional resources, references, or data relevant to real estate compensation

Introduction: The Evolution of Real Estate Compensation

The real estate industry has undergone significant transformations over the decades, evolving in response to economic shifts, technological advancements, and changing consumer expectations. The way real estate professionals are compensated for their services has been central to these changes, reflecting broader trends in the marketplace and in the professional practices within the industry.

Historically, real estate agents have been compensated through commissions—percentage-based fees taken from the final sale price of a property. This model incentivized agents to achieve higher sale prices and facilitated a straightforward, performance-based compensation structure. Traditionally, these commissions have been split between the buyer's and seller's agents, fostering a cooperative environment that benefitted all parties involved.

However, the advent of the internet and digital technology brought about a seismic shift in how properties are listed, viewed, and sold. With an abundance of online resources at their disposal, consumers began to demand more flexibility, transparency, and efficiency in real estate transactions. These demands, coupled with increased scrutiny over traditional commission structures, have spurred innovation within the industry, leading to the exploration of alternative compensation models.

In recent years, discussions around real estate commissions have intensified, culminating in significant legal challenges and settlements, such as the landmark case involving the National Association of Realtors (NAR). These developments have paved the way for a reevaluation of how real estate professionals are compensated, encouraging a move away from the one-size-fits-all commission model towards more diverse and flexible arrangements.

As we delve into the nuances of this evolution, it's essential to recognize the impact of these changes on real estate professionals, consumers, and the industry at large. The shift towards alternative compensation models is not just a response to external pressures but a proactive move towards greater transparency, efficiency, and fairness in real estate transactions. This transformation reflects the industry's resilience and adaptability, as it continues to evolve in the face of changing market dynamics and consumer needs.

The Impact of the NAR Settlement on Traditional Commission Models

The recent settlement involving the National Association of Realtors (NAR) marks a pivotal moment in the real estate industry, with profound implications for traditional commission models. This settlement, arising from a series of legal challenges, questioned the fairness and transparency of the long-standing commission structures in real estate transactions. Its outcomes are poised to reshape the landscape of real estate compensation, challenging industry professionals to adapt to new norms and expectations.

The traditional model, which typically involves commissions of 5% to 6% of the home's sale price being split between the buyer's and seller's agents, has been criticized for lacking transparency and not always aligning with the interests and efforts of real estate professionals. Critics argue that this model does not adequately reflect the varying degrees of work and expertise involved in different transactions, nor does it account for the modern consumer's access to information and preferences for engaging with the real estate market.

The NAR settlement directly addresses these concerns by effectively dismantling policies that mandated the sharing of commissions between listing and buyer's agents. This landmark decision opens the door for more flexible and transparent compensation models, encouraging a shift towards arrangements that can be more closely tailored to the services provided and the value delivered to clients.

Effects on the Industry

Increased Transparency

One of the most immediate impacts of the NAR settlement is the push towards greater transparency in how real estate professionals are compensated. Agents and brokers will need to more clearly communicate the basis of their fees, the services they offer, and the value they provide to their clients.

Rise of Alternative Compensation Models

As outlined in the introduction, the industry is expected to see a rise in alternative compensation models, such as flat fee services, hourly rates, and fee-for-service arrangements. These models offer the potential for more equitable and transparent pricing structures that can be more closely aligned with client needs and service levels.

Consumer Empowerment

The settlement empowers consumers by providing them with more options and flexibility in how they engage with real estate professionals. Buyers and sellers will have the opportunity to negotiate terms that better suit their individual circumstances and preferences, potentially leading to cost savings and improved satisfaction with the real estate process.

Adjustment Period for Professionals

Real estate professionals will face a period of adjustment as they navigate the transition away from traditional commission models. This will require not only a reevaluation of pricing structures but also potentially significant changes to marketing, client engagement strategies, and overall business models.

Regulatory and Legal Landscape

The settlement may also signal a broader shift in the regulatory and legal landscape surrounding real estate transactions. As industry practices evolve in response to the settlement, further legal and regulatory changes could emerge to address new business models and consumer protection concerns.

In summary, the NAR settlement represents a watershed moment for the real estate industry, challenging entrenched norms and catalyzing a shift towards more flexible, transparent, and consumer-friendly compensation models. As the industry adapts to these changes, the ultimate beneficiaries will likely be both real estate professionals, who can tailor their services more precisely to meet client needs, and consumers, who will gain from increased competition, clarity, and choice in the marketplace.

THE MARKET

Homebuyer Search and Internet Usage:

A staggering 97% of homebuyers utilized the internet in their search for a new home.

On average, buyers dedicated eight weeks to their home search, during which they viewed nine homes. Notably, five of these homes were viewed exclusively online.

Real Estate Professional Engagement:

Despite the digital age, a significant 87% of homebuyers enlisted the services of realtors for their purchase.

Real estate agents who leverage video marketing have a competitive edge, with 73% of homeowners expressing a preference to list with agents using video to promote property sales.

Home Sales Data and Predictions:

The National Association of Realtors forecasts a total of 4.71 million existing-home sales in the year 2024.

Recently, the median sales price for an existing home reached $382,600, while new homes commanded a median price of $413,200.

Homebuyer Demographics and Market Dynamics:

The typical first-time homebuyer is now 35 years old, reflecting a demographic shift in the market.

Data from November 2023 indicates that an average homebuyer may need to save for approximately 8.7 years to accumulate a competitive down payment.

Home Search Duration and Preferences:

Approximately half of all homebuyers find their desired property within three months, whereas 13% extend their search from seven months up to a year, based on findings from Zillow Research.

When it comes to home type preferences, 14% of buyers opt for brand new constructions, while a substantial 86% choose homes that have been previously occupied.

Seller Statistics and Market Outcomes:

A loyal 73% of sellers would consider employing the same real estate agent for future transactions.

An overwhelming majority of sellers, 86% to be exact, benefited from the assistance of a real estate agent when selling their property.

The final sale prices matched the original asking price in an impressive 98% of property sales, underscoring the effectiveness of real estate market pricing strategies.

Chapter 1: Flat Fee Services

In the evolving landscape of real estate compensation, flat fee services emerge as a compelling alternative to traditional commission-based models. This chapter delves into the mechanics, benefits, and considerations of flat fee models, offering insights for both real estate professionals and consumers. By adopting a flat fee structure, agents and brokerages can provide transparent, value-focused services, aligning more closely with modern consumer expectations and the shifting regulatory environment highlighted by the NAR settlement.

Understanding Flat Fee Models

Flat fee models represent a departure from the commission-based approach traditionally rooted in the real estate industry. Under a flat fee arrangement, real estate professionals charge a predetermined, fixed amount for their services, regardless of the sale price of the property. This fee covers specific services agreed upon between the agent and the client, which can range from listing the property on MLS to providing full-service support through the sale process.

Key Characteristics of Flat Fee Models:

- **Transparency**

    One of the most significant advantages of flat fee services is the transparency they offer. Clients know exactly how much they will pay upfront, facilitating budget planning and eliminating the uncertainty associated with variable commissions.

- **Cost-Effectiveness**

    For sellers, flat fee services can be more cost-effective, especially for higher-priced properties. Since the fee doesn't scale with the property price, sellers may save money compared to traditional commission percentages.

- **Customization and Flexibility**

    Flat fee models allow for customization of services. Clients can choose a package that best suits their needs, paying only for the services they require. This a la carte approach can appeal to both savvy sellers and those looking for a more guided selling experience.

- **Aligned Interests**

    While traditional commission models incentivize agents to secure the highest sale price, flat fee services focus on the successful completion of the sale itself. This alignment of interests can build trust between clients and agents.

Considerations for Real Estate Professionals:

- **Market Positioning**

    Adopting a flat fee model may require agents to reposition themselves in the market, emphasizing the value, expertise, and specific services they offer rather than competing on commission rates alone.

- **Service Scope Definition**

  Clearly defining the scope of services included in the flat fee is crucial to avoid misunderstandings and ensure clients feel they are receiving value for their investment.

- **Operational Adjustments**

  Shifting to a flat fee model may require changes in how agents and brokerages operate, including adjustments to marketing strategies, client communication, and internal processes to maintain profitability.

- **Regulatory Compliance**

  It's essential to ensure that flat fee arrangements comply with local real estate laws and regulations, particularly in light of the evolving legal landscape post-NAR settlement.

Flat fee models offer an innovative approach to real estate compensation, reflecting the industry's shift towards greater transparency, efficiency, and client-centered service. By understanding the nuances of flat fee services, real estate professionals can adapt to this changing landscape, offering clients clear, upfront pricing and tailored service packages that meet diverse needs and preferences.

Setting Your Flat Fee Structure

Transitioning to a flat fee structure requires careful consideration and strategic planning to ensure that your services are competitively priced, cover your costs, and remain attractive to your target market.

Here are key steps and factors to consider when setting your flat fee structure:

1. **Analyze Your Costs**

   Begin by thoroughly analyzing all costs associated with providing your services. This includes not only direct expenses such as marketing and listing fees but also your time, expertise, and overhead costs. Understanding your cost base is crucial to setting a fee that ensures profitability.

2. **Define Service Packages**

   Decide what services you will offer within your flat fee model. Many agents opt for tiered packages, ranging from basic listing services to full-service support that includes everything from professional photography to closing assistance. Clearly defining each package helps clients understand what they're paying for and allows them to choose the level of service that best suits their needs.

3. **Market Research**

   Research your local market to understand what competitors are charging and the services they offer. This insight will help you price your services competitively and identify any gaps in the market that you could fill with unique offerings.

4. **Consider Your Target Market**

   Your pricing should reflect the needs and expectations of your target market. For example, if you're targeting high-end property sellers, they may expect more comprehensive services and be willing to pay a premium for them. Conversely, if your target market is budget-conscious sellers, your services and pricing should cater to their needs for cost-effectiveness and efficiency.

5. **Price for Value**

   When setting your fees, consider the value you bring to your clients. Your pricing should reflect your expertise, the quality of your services, and the benefits clients receive from working with you. Communicating this value effectively can justify your fees and differentiate you from competitors who may simply be competing on price.

6. **Feedback and Adjustment**

   After launching your flat fee services, seek feedback from clients to understand their perceptions of the value they received. Be prepared to adjust your packages or pricing based on this feedback and market changes to remain competitive and meet client needs.

7. **Transparency is Key**

   Ensure that your pricing and what's included in each package are transparent and clearly communicated in your marketing materials and client interactions. This transparency builds trust and helps set realistic expectations, reducing the potential for misunderstandings and dissatisfaction.

8. **Legal Compliance:**

   Verify that your flat fee structure complies with local real estate regulations and laws. It's crucial to maintain compliance to avoid any legal issues that could arise from improper fee disclosure or services rendered.

Setting a flat fee structure is a strategic process that requires a deep understanding of your costs, market, and target clientele. By considering these factors and focusing on the value you provide, you can create a compelling, competitive offering that appeals to modern consumers looking for transparency and fairness in real estate transactions.

Benefits and Challenges for Agents and Clients

The shift towards flat fee services in real estate brings a mix of benefits and challenges, both for agents and their clients. Understanding these can help both parties make informed decisions and set realistic expectations.

Benefits for Agents

- **Predictable Income**

    Flat fee services allow agents to predict their income more accurately based on the number of transactions, rather than the variable nature of commission percentages.

- **Market Differentiation**

    Offering flat fee services can help agents stand out in a competitive market by appealing to cost-conscious sellers or those seeking clear, upfront pricing.

- **Efficiency Gains**

    By standardizing services, agents can streamline their operations, potentially handling more transactions with the same level of resources.

Challenges for Agents

- **Perceived Value**

    Convincing sellers of the value of a flat fee service, especially when compared to traditional commission models, can be challenging. Agents must clearly articulate the benefits and justify their fees.

- **Revenue Fluctuations**

    In high-value property markets, agents might earn less from a flat fee than they would from a percentage-based commission, affecting overall revenue.

- **Service Scope Management**

    Strictly defining and adhering to the scope of services included in a flat fee can be difficult, especially with clients who expect additional support without extra charges.

Benefits for Clients

- **Cost Savings**

    For sellers, especially of higher-priced homes, flat fee services can offer significant cost savings compared to traditional commissions.

- **Transparency and Simplicity**

    Clients appreciate knowing exactly what they will pay upfront, making budgeting easier and eliminating surprises at closing.

- **Customization**

    Clients can choose services based on their needs, potentially reducing costs by only paying for what they really need.

Challenges for Clients

- **Understanding Service Limits**

    Clients may not fully grasp the limitations of a flat fee service package and might expect more comprehensive support than what's covered.

- **Finding the Right Fit**

    Not all agents offer flat fee services, and among those who do, finding the right package and agent fit for a seller's specific needs can take time.

- **Quality Concerns**

    There may be concerns about the quality of service, as some may perceive that a lower fee equals lesser service, though this is not necessarily the case.

Overcoming Challenges

- **Clear Communication**

    Both agents and clients must maintain open lines of communication, with agents providing clear explanations of what their services include and clients expressing their expectations and needs.

- **Flexibility and Customization**

    Offering customizable packages can help address the diverse needs of clients, allowing them to add services for additional fees.

- **Education and Transparency**

    Agents should educate their clients about the real estate process and how flat fee structures work, including the potential benefits and limitations, to set realistic expectations.

The flat fee model represents a significant shift in real estate, providing benefits like cost savings and transparency for clients while offering agents a way to diversify their services and income. However, success in this model relies on clear communication, understanding the market, and setting appropriate expectations from the outset.

Case Studies: Success Stories and Lessons Learned

In this section, we explore various case studies from the real estate industry that highlight the successes and challenges of implementing flat fee services. Through these examples, we can glean valuable insights and best practices for both agents considering this model and clients navigating their options.

- Case Study 1: The Efficient Marketer

  A real estate agent in a bustling metropolitan area implemented a flat fee service that streamlined the listing and selling process for condos and apartments. By offering a comprehensive package that included professional photography, listing services, and negotiation support for a fixed price, the agent was able to attract a high volume of clients looking for straightforward, cost-effective solutions.

  Lesson Learned: Efficiency and clear value propositions are key. This agent succeeded by offering a service that met a specific market need, ensuring that the scope of services was well-defined and communicated.

- Case Study 2: The Value Communicator

  In a suburban community, another agent faced initial skepticism about the value of flat fee services compared to traditional commission models. By meticulously documenting and sharing the outcomes of their flat fee listings, including how much money sellers saved, the agent built a compelling case that attracted more clients over time.

  Lesson Learned: Transparency and evidence-based marketing can overcome skepticism. Showing potential clients the tangible benefits and savings can shift perceptions about the value of flat fee services.

- Case Study 3: The Customizer

  A real estate professional specializing in luxury homes offered a flat fee model with customizable options, allowing clients to add on services a la carte. This approach catered to high-end clients who valued both the base level of service and the flexibility to enhance their package.

Lesson Learned: Flexibility and customization can broaden your client base. Providing options allows clients to tailor services to their needs, enhancing satisfaction and perceived value.

- **Case Study 4: The Niche Expert**

    One agent focused exclusively on representing buyers in a competitive market and offered flat fee rebates to clients. This unique approach not only differentiated them from other buyer's agents but also passed on savings to clients, who often felt overlooked in the traditional commission model.

    Lesson Learned: Finding a niche and offering specialized services can set you apart. This strategy can attract clients who feel underserved by the current market, building loyalty and referrals.

- **Case Study 5: The Community Educator**

    Facing initial resistance to flat fee models, an agent embarked on a local education campaign, holding seminars and online webinars to explain how flat fee services work and the potential benefits. This effort not only demystified the model for many but also positioned the agent as a trusted community resource.

    Lesson Learned: Education can be a powerful tool in changing market dynamics. By investing in community education, agents can build trust and interest in alternative service models.

These case studies demonstrate that while transitioning to a flat fee model presents challenges, there are also significant opportunities for agents willing to innovate and adapt. Key to these successes are clear communication, understanding client needs, and demonstrating the value and savings that can be achieved. As the real estate industry continues to evolve, these lessons can guide both new and experienced professionals in navigating the changing landscape.

Flat Fee
Sample

Package	Description	Flat Fee
Basic Listing Package	Includes MLS listing, property photos (up to 25), and listing description.	$1,000
Enhanced Marketing Package	Basic Listing Package plus professional home staging consultation, premium photography, and targeted online advertising campaign.	$2,500
Comprehensive Seller's Package	Enhanced Marketing Package plus virtual tours, open house coordination, and negotiation support.	$5,000
Buyer's Representation Package	Includes property search, personalized showings (up to 10 properties), offer preparation, and negotiation support.	$3,000
Investment Analysis Package	Market analysis, investment property identification, ROI calculations, and personalized investment strategy consultation.	$1,500
A La Carte Services	Options include single property showing ($100), contract review ($250), pricing analysis ($200), etc. Pricing per service.	Varies

When implementing hourly rates, clear communication and documentation are vital. Consider using time-tracking software to accurately log hours worked and provide detailed invoices to clients, breaking down the services rendered and time spent on each task. This transparency fosters trust and can lead to more satisfied clients.

Chapter 2: Hourly Rates

In a real estate industry traditionally dominated by commission-based compensation, the concept of hourly rates presents a groundbreaking shift. This chapter delves into the hourly billing model, exploring how it aligns with contemporary demands for transparency and fairness in professional services. By charging clients for the actual time spent on their transaction, real estate professionals offer an alternative that can appeal to a wide range of clients, from those engaging in more straightforward transactions to those requiring extensive, specialized services.

Transitioning to Hourly Billing in Real Estate

Transitioning to an hourly billing model in real estate involves a significant shift in both mindset and business operations. This section outlines the steps and considerations for real estate professionals considering this model, highlighting the potential benefits and challenges of such a transition.

- *Understanding the Model*

    Hourly billing means charging clients for the exact time spent working on their behalf. This can range from consultations and market analysis to property showings and transaction management. The key is to log hours accurately and communicate the value of these services effectively.

- *Setting Hourly Rates*

    Determining an appropriate hourly rate requires an analysis of your expertise, the complexity of services offered, and market standards. It's essential to find a balance that reflects your value but remains competitive and accessible to your target clients.

- **Communicating Value**

    Shifting to hourly rates demands clear communication with clients about the benefits of this model. It's crucial to articulate how paying for actual time spent can lead to cost savings and more personalized services.

- **Operational Adjustments**

    Implementing hourly billing requires operational changes, including time tracking and invoicing systems. Agents must be meticulous about recording their hours and transparent in reporting them to clients.

- **Client Contracts**

    Contracts or agreements outlining the hourly rate model, services provided, and billing procedures are vital. These documents ensure clarity and agreement from both parties, reducing potential disputes over billing.

- **Navigating Challenges**

    Transitioning to hourly billing may meet resistance from those accustomed to traditional commission models. Overcoming this hurdle involves educating clients on the benefits and ensuring they understand the value of the services they are receiving.

- **Market Positioning**

    Successfully adopting an hourly rate model may require repositioning in the market. This could involve targeting clients who value transparency and are comfortable with a more consultative approach to real estate transactions.

- **Benefits and Limitations**

    While hourly billing offers greater transparency and can align costs more directly with services rendered, it may not be suitable for all transactions or clients.

Understanding these dynamics is critical for real estate professionals considering this model.

Transitioning to hourly billing in real estate represents a significant departure from traditional practices. However, for professionals willing to navigate the challenges, it offers an opportunity to cater to a market segment increasingly seeking transparency, fairness, and direct alignment of fees with services provided. This model not only has the potential to enhance client satisfaction but also to redefine the value proposition of real estate services in a changing industry landscape.

How to Determine Your Hourly Rate

Determining your hourly rate as a real estate professional involves a careful assessment of several key factors to ensure your rate is competitive, fair, and reflective of your value.

Here are the steps and considerations to guide you in setting an appropriate hourly rate:

- **Assess Your Costs**

    Begin by calculating your operating costs, including overhead expenses (office space, utilities, marketing, software subscriptions, professional fees, etc.), as well as the direct costs associated with providing services to clients. Understanding your cost base is crucial to ensuring that your hourly rate covers these expenses and leaves room for profit.

- **Evaluate Your Experience and Expertise**

    Your level of experience and expertise in the real estate industry significantly impacts your value to clients. More experienced agents, those with specialized knowledge, or certifications can justifiably charge higher rates. Consider your track record, the complexity of transactions you handle, and any niche areas of expertise when setting your rate.

- **Analyze Market Rates**

    Research what other real estate professionals in your area and niche are charging for similar services. This information helps you position your rate competitively while ensuring it aligns with market expectations. Keep in mind that rates can vary widely based on geographic location, the type of real estate services offered, and the target client base.

- **Consider the Scope of Services**

    Reflect on the range of services you plan to offer on an hourly basis. More comprehensive and specialized services can command higher rates. Clearly defining what each hour of work entails helps justify your rates to clients and sets clear expectations for what they receive in exchange for their investment.

- **Factor in Demand and Availability**

    Your workload and demand for your services can influence your hourly rate. If you are in high demand, you might adjust your rate upwards to manage workload and ensure quality service. Conversely, if you're looking to attract more clients, a competitive rate can be a strategic choice.

- **Set Goals for Income**

    Consider your income goals and how many billable hours you aim to work each week or month. Setting an hourly rate that helps you achieve these income targets, while remaining realistic about market conditions and demand for your services, is essential.

- **Create a Tiered Structure**

    For agents offering a range of services, consider implementing a tiered pricing structure with different rates for various services. Routine tasks might be billed at a standard rate, while more complex or specialized services could command a premium.

- **Trial and Feedback**

    After setting your hourly rate, be open to adjusting it based on feedback, market changes, and your evolving experience level. Regularly revisiting and adjusting your rate ensures it remains competitive and reflective of your current value in the market.

Determining your hourly rate is a dynamic process that balances internal costs, market conditions, and the unique value you offer to clients. By carefully considering these factors, you can set a rate that is fair, competitive, and aligned with your business goals and client expectations.

Managing Client Expectations and Billing Transparency

Successfully implementing an hourly billing model in real estate hinges on effectively managing client expectations and maintaining billing transparency. This section outlines strategies to ensure that clients understand and are comfortable with this compensation structure, fostering trust and a positive working relationship.

- **Educate Your Clients**

    Begin by educating clients about the hourly billing model, emphasizing its benefits such as cost control and payment only for services rendered. Explain how this model can offer flexibility and potentially lower costs compared to traditional commission-based models. Use examples or scenarios to illustrate how hourly billing works in practice.

- **Clear Communication from the Start**

    At the onset of your client relationship, clearly communicate your hourly rate, the services included, and any other billing policies. Discuss how you track your time and how often they can expect to receive updates or invoices. Setting these expectations early helps prevent misunderstandings and establishes a foundation of transparency.

- **Detailed Time Tracking**

    Implement a reliable system for tracking the time you spend on each client's activities. Use tools or software that allow you to record tasks accurately and provide detailed descriptions of the work performed. This not only ensures you're compensated fairly but also builds client trust by showing exactly where their investment goes.

- **Regular Billing Updates**

    Provide clients with regular updates on their billable hours, ideally before sending an invoice. Consider setting up weekly or bi-weekly check-ins to review the hours spent and discuss ongoing activities. This keeps clients informed about their expenses and allows for adjustments in service as needed.

- **Transparent Invoicing**

    Ensure that your invoices are detailed, clearly listing the dates, tasks performed, time spent on each task, and the total cost. Transparency in invoicing reassures clients about the fairness of billing and reduces the likelihood of disputes.

- **Address Concerns Promptly**

    Be prepared to address any client concerns about billing or the perceived value of your services promptly. Listen to their feedback and be willing to adjust your approach if necessary to maintain a positive relationship.

- **Value Proposition**

    Consistently remind clients of the value you bring to their real estate transactions. Whether it's your expertise, market knowledge, negotiation skills, or the personalized attention you offer, make sure they understand the benefits of working with you on an hourly basis.

- **Client Empowerment**

    Empower clients by involving them in the decision-making process about how your time is spent. This can include prioritizing certain tasks or setting a cap on hours for specific activities. Giving clients a say in these decisions enhances their sense of control and satisfaction with the services provided.

Managing client expectations and billing transparency is critical to the success of an hourly billing model in real estate. By employing these strategies, real estate professionals can foster trust, reduce the potential for billing disputes, and highlight the value of their expertise and services, leading to more satisfied clients and successful business outcomes.

Real-Life Applications: When Hourly Rates Work Best

The hourly billing model in real estate is not a one-size-fits-all solution but shines in specific scenarios where its advantages can be fully leveraged. Understanding when and how to apply this model can enhance the value offered to clients while ensuring fair compensation for services rendered.

Here are several real-life applications where hourly rates work best:

1. **Consultation and Advisory Services**

   Clients seeking professional advice on real estate investments, market analysis, or property valuation can benefit significantly from an hourly rate model. This arrangement is particularly suited for clients who require expert guidance but are not yet committed to buying or selling.

2. **Specialized Real Estate Transactions**

   Transactions involving unique properties (such as historical homes, commercial real estate, or overseas properties) often require specialized knowledge and extensive research. An hourly rate model compensates agents for the additional expertise and time these transactions demand.

3. **Client Education and Market Analysis**

   First-time homebuyers or sellers, investors new to a specific market, or clients looking to understand the complexities of real estate transactions can benefit from educational sessions billed at an hourly rate. This model allows clients to access tailored education and market insights without the commitment of a full-service package.

4. **Negotiation and Closing Support**

   Clients who have handled most of the transaction process themselves but require professional support for negotiation and closing can engage a real estate professional on an hourly basis. This targeted assistance ensures clients receive expert support only where needed, optimizing their investment.

5. **Property Search and Screening**

   For clients who prefer to conduct their property search but need a professional's input on selecting and screening potential properties, hourly billing can be ideal. This service can include reviewing listings, advising on property potential, and accompanying clients on select viewings.

Hourly Rate
Sample

Services Category	Hourly Rate
General Consultation - Market analysis, general advice, and strategy sessions.	$75 - $150
Specialized Consultation - Investment strategy, property development advice, and legal considerations.	$100 - $200
Propery Listing Services - Preparing and managing listings, including descriptions and basic photography.	$50 - $100
Marketing and Promotion - Creating and executing marketing plans, professional photography, and virtual tours.	$100 - $150
Property Showing Assistance - Organizing and conducting property showings for buyers or renters.	$50 - $100
Transaction and Negotiation Support - Assistance with offers, negotiations, and closing procedures.	$100 - $200
Paperwork and Compliance - Preparing, reviewing, and managing necessary documentation and ensuring compliance.	$75 - $150

When implementing hourly rates, clear communication and documentation are vital. Consider using time-tracking software to accurately log hours worked and provide detailed invoices to clients, breaking down the services rendered and time spent on each task. This transparency fosters trust and can lead to more satisfied clients.

Key Considerations for Setting Hourly Rates

1. **Experience and Expertise:** Rates should reflect your level of experience and area of expertise. Specialists or highly experienced agents can command higher rates.
2. **Service Complexity:** More complex services that require specialized knowledge or skills should have higher rates to reflect the added value provided.
3. **Market Standards:** Research the going rates in your area for similar services to ensure your pricing is competitive and fair.
4. **Client Expectations:** Be transparent about your rates and how you track your time. Providing estimates on hours for specific tasks can help manage client expectations.

Chapter 3: Fee for Service

In the evolving landscape of real estate compensation, the Fee for Service (FFS) model stands out as a versatile and client-centered approach. This chapter explores the nuances of the FFS model, which allows real estate professionals to offer their services a la carte, enabling clients to pay only for the specific services they need. This model contrasts sharply with the traditional commission-based system, offering potential cost savings and increased flexibility for clients, while also presenting unique challenges and opportunities for agents.

Breaking Down the Fee for Service Model

The Fee for Service model in real estate breaks down the selling or buying process into individual tasks or services, each with its own set price. This model allows clients to customize the real estate service package according to their specific needs, offering a transparent and potentially more economical alternative to the traditional percentage-based commission model.

Key Components of the FFS Model:

- **A La Carte Services**

    The core of the FFS model is its menu of services, which might include listing the property on MLS, professional photography, open house coordination, marketing, negotiation assistance, paperwork handling, and closing support. Clients can select and pay for only the services they require.

- **Transparency and Flexibility**

  This model promotes transparency, as clients know exactly what each service costs upfront. It also offers flexibility, accommodating clients who may only need partial services because they can handle some aspects of the transaction themselves.

- **Customization**

  FFS allows for high levels of customization, catering to a diverse clientele with varying needs, from sellers who only need help listing their property to buyers who want support during the negotiation and closing phases.

Advantages of the FFS Model:

- **Cost Efficiency**

  Clients can save money by only paying for the services they need, which can be particularly appealing in straightforward transactions or for clients with previous real estate experience.

- **Empowerment**

  The model empowers clients by giving them control over the services they use and the costs associated with their real estate transactions.

- **Market Adaptability**

  Real estate professionals can adapt their offerings to meet market demands, providing services that clients value and are willing to pay for.

Challenges of the FFS Model:

- **Revenue Predictability**

    For agents, revenue can be less predictable compared to the traditional commission model, as income is directly tied to the volume and type of services rendered.

- **Service Scope**

    Defining the scope of each service and managing client expectations can be challenging, requiring clear communication and detailed service agreements.

- **Market Education**

    Educating the market about the benefits and structure of the FFS model can require significant effort, as it represents a departure from the traditional way of conducting real estate transactions.

The Fee for Service model presents an innovative approach to real estate transactions, aligning with modern consumers' desires for transparency, customization, and control. As the real estate market continues to evolve, the FFS model offers both challenges and opportunities for professionals looking to meet the changing needs and expectations of their clients.

Itemizing Your Real Estate Services

In the Fee for Service (FFS) model, itemizing real estate services involves breaking down the entire process of buying or selling property into distinct tasks or services that can be individually selected and paid for by the client. This section outlines how real estate professionals can effectively itemize their services, offering clarity and flexibility to clients while ensuring a comprehensive approach to real estate transactions.

Defining Services Clearly

Start by categorizing your services into logical groups such as pre-listing, listing, marketing, negotiation, closing, and post-closing services. Each category should include specific tasks that are essential to the real estate process. For example, pre-listing services might encompass market analysis, property valuation, and staging advice.

Examples of Itemized Services

- *Market Analysis and Property Valuation*

    Offering detailed market research and property valuation to help sellers price their homes competitively or assist buyers in understanding potential investments.

- *Listing Services*

    Including MLS listing, creating property descriptions, and ensuring listings are syndicated across relevant real estate platforms.

- *Marketing Package*

    Crafting a comprehensive marketing strategy that may involve professional photography, virtual tours, social media promotion, and traditional advertising.

- *Open House Coordination*

    Managing the logistics of open houses, including scheduling, signage, and follow-up with attendees.

- **Negotiation Assistance**

    Providing expertise during offer negotiation to ensure favorable terms for the client.

- **Paperwork and Compliance**

    Ensuring all necessary paperwork is accurately completed, and regulatory compliance is maintained throughout the transaction process.

- **Closing Support**

    Assisting with closing logistics, including coordinating with closing agents, ensuring all financial transactions are in order, and addressing any last-minute issues.

Pricing Strategies

For each service, develop a pricing strategy that reflects the time, expertise, and resources required. Pricing can vary based on market norms, the complexity of the service, and your level of expertise. Offering packages that bundle services together at a discounted rate can also appeal to clients looking for a more comprehensive service selection.

Communicating Value

Clearly communicate the value of each service to potential clients. This involves explaining how each service contributes to the success of their real estate transaction, the expertise you bring to the table, and how your services can save them time and money or increase their profitability.

Customization and Flexibility

Allow for customization of services based on client needs. Some clients may only need assistance with certain aspects of their transaction, while others may prefer a more comprehensive package. Offering the flexibility to choose services a la carte or in pre-defined packages can cater to a broad range of client preferences.

Transparency and Documentation

Provide detailed descriptions and transparent pricing for each service in your marketing materials, on your website, and in client agreements. Clear documentation helps manage expectations and reduces the potential for disputes, fostering trust and satisfaction among your clients.

Itemizing your real estate services under the FFS model not only enhances transparency and flexibility but also empowers clients to tailor the real estate process to their specific needs. By clearly defining and pricing each service, real estate professionals can cater to a diverse clientele, ensuring both parties achieve their objectives in an efficient and mutually beneficial manner.

Strategies for Marketing a Menu of Services

Marketing a menu of real estate services effectively is key to attracting a broad clientele and ensuring that potential clients understand the value and flexibility offered by the Fee for Service (FFS) model.

Here are strategies for marketing your diverse range of services:

1. **Leverage Digital Platforms**

   Website: Your website should serve as the central hub for information about your services. Create a dedicated section for your menu of services, including detailed descriptions, pricing, and the benefits of each service. Incorporate client testimonials and case studies to showcase your success stories.

   Social Media: Utilize social media platforms to highlight different aspects of your services. Regular posts can cover topics like the benefits of individual services, behind-the-scenes looks at how you work, and success stories.

2. **Content Marketing**

   Develop informative content that positions you as a thought leader in the real estate industry. Blog posts, eBooks, and videos can cover topics relevant to your services, offering insights into the real estate process, tips for buyers and sellers, and the advantages of the FFS model.

3. **Targeted Email Campaigns**

   Segment your email list to target specific groups with tailored messages. For example, you could send information about your listing services to potential sellers and details about your negotiation and closing support services to buyers.

4. **Educational Workshops and Seminars**

   Host free or low-cost workshops and seminars, either in-person or online, to educate potential clients about the real estate process and the benefits of choosing services a la carte. These events provide an excellent opportunity to showcase your expertise and market your services directly to interested individuals.

5. **Partnerships and Networking**

   Collaborate with local businesses, financial advisors, and legal professionals to cross-promote your services. Networking events and professional associations can also be valuable venues for promoting your menu of services to a wider audience.

6. **Client Reviews and Testimonials**

   Positive reviews and testimonials from satisfied clients are powerful marketing tools. Encourage clients to leave reviews on your website, social media profiles, and online directories. Highlighting specific services that clients found valuable can attract others looking for similar support.

7. **Customized Service Packages**

   Offer pre-designed packages of commonly bundled services at a slightly discounted rate to simplify the decision-making process for clients. Marketing these packages alongside your a la carte options provides flexibility while also catering to clients who prefer a more straightforward choice.

8. **Clear Communication of Value**

   Ensure that all marketing materials clearly communicate the value and benefits of each service. Use language that speaks to the client's needs, focusing on how your services can save them time, money, and stress.

By implementing these strategies, real estate professionals can effectively market their menu of services, attracting a diverse range of clients and differentiating themselves in a competitive market. The key is to communicate the value, flexibility, and personalized nature of the Fee for Service model, making it a compelling choice for prospective clients navigating the real estate process.

Client Perspectives: Customizing Their Experience

Customizing the real estate experience through a Fee for Service (FFS) model resonates deeply with clients' desire for control, transparency, and tailored services. This section explores how clients view and benefit from the ability to customize their real estate services, reflecting on the positive impacts of this model from their perspective.

Empowerment Through Choice

Clients often feel more empowered when they can choose exactly which services they need. This empowerment comes from the understanding that they're not paying for a one-size-fits-all package but rather for services that directly address their unique situation and goals. The ability to tailor services to their precise needs can lead to greater satisfaction with the real estate process.

Financial Transparency and Savings

One of the most appreciated aspects of the FFS model from a client's perspective is financial transparency. Knowing the cost of each service upfront helps clients budget more effectively and avoid surprises. Moreover, by paying only for services they require, clients can potentially achieve significant savings, especially if they are knowledgeable about some aspects of the real estate process and can handle them independently.

Enhanced Trust and Relationship

The customization and transparency inherent in the FFS model can enhance trust between clients and real estate professionals. When clients see that their agent is willing to work within a structure that potentially reduces the agent's income in favor of what's best for the client, it builds a foundation of trust and mutual respect. This positive relationship dynamic can lead to repeat business and referrals.

Appreciation for Specialized Expertise

Clients value the opportunity to engage real estate professionals for their specialized expertise. Whether it's market analysis, negotiation skills, or handling complex paperwork, clients recognize the value of expert assistance in specific areas. The FFS model allows them to access this expertise in a more flexible and cost-effective manner than traditional commissions might permit.

Tailored Support for Unique Needs

Every real estate transaction is unique, and clients appreciate when services are adapted to their specific circumstances. For example, clients dealing with unique properties or challenging market conditions might require more specialized services that a standard commission-based model might not adequately compensate an agent for. The FFS model's flexibility ensures that these clients receive the focused attention and expertise they need.

Streamlined Services for Experienced Clients

Experienced buyers and sellers, such as investors or those who have been through the real estate process multiple times, often have specific requirements and may not need the full suite of services offered by agents. These clients particularly appreciate the ability to streamline their service package to exclude steps they're comfortable handling on their own, thereby optimizing their expenditure on professional services.

From the client's perspective, the Fee for Service model offers a refreshing alternative to traditional real estate transactions. It aligns with modern consumers' expectations for transparency, customization, and control, enhancing their overall experience and satisfaction with the real estate process. As this model continues to gain traction, understanding and catering to client perspectives on customization will be key for real estate professionals aiming to provide exceptional service and build lasting relationships.

Fee for Service
Sample

	Services Offered	Price Range
Pre-Listing Services	Market Analysis and Property Valuation	$150 - $500
	Home Staging Consultation	$100 - $300
	Professional Photography	$200 - $600
Listing Services	MLS Listing Setup	$150 - $350
	Listing Description and Marketing Material	$100 - $400
Marketing Package	Social Media and Online Advertising	$250 - $750
	Open House Coordination	$150 - $500
Transaction Services	Negotiation Assistance	$300 - $1,000
	Paperwork and Compliance Handling	$200 - $600
	Closing Support	$300 - $800
Pre-closing Services	Assistance with Post-Closing Issues	$100 - $300
	Property Management Consultation	$150 - $500

Please note, the prices listed are hypothetical and are intended to serve as a starting point for real estate professionals considering the FFS model. Factors such as the complexity of services, the real estate professional's experience level, and local market rates should be considered when determining actual pricing.

Chapter 4: Retainer Plus Success Fee

The retainer plus success fee model offers a hybrid approach to real estate compensation that combines the upfront commitment of a retainer with the performance-based incentive of a success fee. This model aligns the interests of real estate professionals and their clients towards a common goal: the successful sale or purchase of property. By providing a more predictable income for agents and more transparent costs for clients, this approach addresses some of the uncertainties inherent in purely commission-based models.

The Hybrid Approach: Retainer and Success Fees Explained

The retainer plus success fee model is a two-part compensation structure designed to balance the immediate effort required by real estate professionals with the ultimate outcome of their services.

Retainer Fee

This is an upfront fee paid by the client to the real estate professional at the beginning of their working relationship. The retainer covers the initial costs and efforts associated with getting the property ready for sale or beginning the search for a property to purchase. It ensures that the agent is compensated for their time and expenses, regardless of the transaction's outcome. The retainer fee can vary significantly based on the scope of services provided, market conditions, and the agent's expertise.

Success Fee

The success fee is contingent upon the successful conclusion of a real estate transaction — typically the sale of a property. It is often a percentage of the sale price, similar to traditional commission models, but can be reduced in consideration of the retainer already paid. This fee structure incentivizes agents to successfully close deals, as their more substantial compensation is contingent upon a successful outcome.

Advantages of the Hybrid Model:

- **Predictability for Agents**

    The retainer provides a predictable stream of income that helps agents manage their finances, especially during periods when sales might be slow.

- **Motivation to Close**

    The success fee motivates agents to close the deal, ensuring that their interests are aligned with those of their clients.

- **Transparency and Trust**

    Clients appreciate the transparency of knowing part of their costs upfront and understanding that their agent has a vested interest in achieving a successful sale.

- **Flexibility**

    This model offers flexibility to adjust the retainer and success fee based on the complexity of the transaction, the level of service required, and other specific client needs.

Challenges of the Hybrid Model:

- ***Initial Client Buy-in***

    Convincing clients to pay an upfront retainer can be challenging, especially in markets where this model is not common.

- ***Determining the Appropriate Fees***

    Setting the right level for both the retainer and the success fee requires careful consideration to ensure competitiveness while also reflecting the value of the services provided.

Implementing a retainer plus success fee model requires clear communication with clients about the benefits and structure of this compensation approach. Real estate professionals should articulate how this model provides them with the financial stability to dedicate the necessary time and resources to serve their clients effectively while also keeping their interests aligned with achieving a successful transaction. This model represents a strategic approach to real estate compensation, offering an innovative alternative to traditional fee structures.

Calculating Retainers and Success Fees

The hybrid compensation model of retainer plus success fee in real estate strikes a balance between securing an initial commitment from the client and ensuring the agent is motivated to see the transaction through to a successful conclusion. Here's how to approach calculating both components:

Setting the Retainer Fee

- **Assess Initial Efforts and Costs**

    Estimate the initial work and costs involved in the early stages of the service. This could include market analysis, property preparation advice, initial listings, and marketing efforts for sellers, or property search and initial viewings for buyers.

- **Determine an Hourly Rate or Fixed Cost**

    Depending on the expected effort, calculate the retainer by applying either an hourly rate for your time or a fixed cost that covers the initial services. This rate or cost should reflect your expertise, the anticipated hours of work, and any direct expenses you'll incur.

- **Consider Market Standards**

    Research the typical retainers charged in your market for similar services to ensure your rates are competitive yet fair. This research can help you position your retainer fee attractively while ensuring it covers your value.

- **Communicate Value Clearly**

    Be prepared to explain what the retainer covers and why it's required. Clients are more likely to agree to a retainer if they understand the immediate benefits and the work you'll undertake on their behalf.

Calculating the Success Fee

- **Percentage of the Sale Price**

    The success fee is typically a percentage of the final sale price. Determine a rate that reflects the value of your full range of services minus the retainer already paid. This rate should be competitive with traditional commission structures but account for the upfront retainer.

- **Adjust for the Retainer**

    Consider the retainer as a prepayment towards the total commission. For example, if you would normally charge a 6% commission and the retainer was $2,000, you might reduce the success fee to ensure the total cost (retainer + success fee) aligns with market norms or reflects a discount for the upfront payment.

- **Performance Incentives**

    Some agents include performance incentives in their success fee structure, such as a slightly lower percentage for achieving a sale within a specific timeframe or exceeding a certain sale price. This can align incentives further and reassure clients of your commitment to their goals.

- **Transparent Agreement**

    Ensure that the retainer and success fee agreement is clearly outlined in your contract with the client, including how the retainer is credited towards the success fee and under what circumstances the success fee is earned.

Calculating retainers and success fees requires a balance between covering your initial efforts and remaining competitive and fair. By carefully assessing your costs, understanding the value you provide, and communicating effectively with clients, you can implement a retainer plus success fee model that benefits both you and your clients, fostering a positive and productive working relationship.

Balancing Upfront Costs with Final Rewards

Balancing the upfront costs associated with a retainer against the potential final rewards of a success fee requires strategic planning and clear communication with clients. This balance is essential for maintaining a positive relationship with clients while ensuring the real estate professional is fairly compensated for their efforts. Here are key strategies for achieving this balance:

Understanding Value and Costs

- **Comprehensive Service Analysis**

    Begin by thoroughly analyzing the services you provide, including both the initial efforts covered by the retainer and the full scope of work anticipated to successfully close a transaction. This analysis helps in accurately pricing the retainer and success fee.

- **Transparent Cost Breakdown**

    Offer clients a clear breakdown of what the retainer covers and how it contributes to the overall success of the transaction. Highlighting the specific activities and associated costs can help clients appreciate the value they're receiving upfront.

Strategic Retainer Setting

- **Fair Pricing**

    Set a retainer fee that fairly compensates for the initial phase of work without deterring potential clients. The retainer should reflect the value of your expertise and the direct costs of initiating the real estate process.

- **Flexible Retainer Options**

    Consider offering different retainer levels based on the scope of services required by the client. This flexibility can accommodate varying client needs and budgets, making the retainer plus success fee model more accessible.

Aligning Success Fees with Client Goals

- **Outcome-Based Success Fees**

    Structure the success fee to reflect the achievement of client goals, such as securing a sale within a certain price range or timeframe. This alignment ensures that both the client and the agent are working towards a common objective, enhancing motivation and satisfaction.

- **Adjusting for Market Dynamics**

    Regularly review and adjust your success fee structure to reflect current market conditions and trends. This adaptability ensures that your fees remain competitive and fair, aligning with client expectations and market standards.

Enhancing Client Relationships

- **Open Communication**

    Maintain open lines of communication with clients throughout the transaction process. Regular updates on progress and discussions about any adjustments to strategy or pricing reinforce trust and transparency.

- **Highlighting Long-Term Benefits**

    Emphasize the long-term benefits of the retainer plus success fee model, such as personalized service, aligned incentives, and potentially lower overall costs compared to traditional commission structures.

Ensuring Fair Compensation

- **Performance Incentives**

    Incorporate performance incentives into the success fee to ensure that exceptional results are appropriately rewarded. This approach can motivate real estate professionals to exceed client expectations while providing additional value.

- **Clear Contracts**

    Ensure all agreements clearly articulate the terms of the retainer, success fee, and any conditions or performance benchmarks associated with compensation. A well-drafted contract prevents misunderstandings and strengthens the professional-client relationship.

Balancing upfront costs with final rewards in the retainer plus success fee model involves a combination of strategic pricing, clear communication, and alignment of incentives. By carefully considering both the immediate value provided to clients and the ultimate success of real estate transactions, real estate professionals can implement this hybrid compensation model effectively, ensuring both client satisfaction and fair compensation for their efforts.

Success Stories: Maximizing Earnings While Providing Value

The retainer plus success fee model in real estate has led to numerous success stories where professionals have maximized their earnings while providing exceptional value to their clients. These stories illustrate the model's effectiveness in aligning the interests of real estate agents and their clients, leading to successful transactions and satisfied parties. Below are synthesized narratives based on common outcomes and feedback from those who have adopted this hybrid compensation model.

The Efficient Closer

A real estate professional, specializing in high-end properties, transitioned to the retainer plus success fee model to better align their efforts with their compensation. By setting a reasonable retainer, they covered initial marketing and listing costs, ensuring their upfront efforts were compensated. The success fee was structured to reward the agent for securing offers above the asking price. This model motivated the agent to leverage their extensive network and marketing skills, resulting in faster sales and higher prices. The agent's earnings increased by 20% in the first year of adopting this model, demonstrating its effectiveness in incentivizing high-performance while providing clients with transparent and value-driven services.

The Market Educator

Another agent found success by focusing on educating their clients about the benefits of the retainer plus success fee model. They developed informative materials and workshops that clearly explained how the model works, its benefits, and how it compares to traditional commission structures. This educational approach helped demystify the model for clients and resulted in a higher acceptance rate. The clarity and upfront nature of the retainer built trust with clients, and the success fee ensured the agent remained fully committed to achieving the best possible outcome for their clients. This approach led to increased client satisfaction, referrals, and a significant boost in the agent's annual income.

The Niche Specialist

Recognizing the unique needs of clients looking to buy or sell properties in niche markets, such as eco-friendly homes or properties in rural areas, one agent tailored their retainer plus success fee model to offer specialized services. The retainer covered the cost of targeted marketing campaigns and personalized property searches, while the success fee incentivized the agent to find the perfect match for their clients' specific needs. This specialization allowed the agent to command a higher retainer and success fee due to their unique expertise, resulting in higher earnings and establishing the agent as a go-to expert in their niche market.

The Flexible Negotiator

An agent who primarily worked with first-time homebuyers introduced a sliding scale for their retainer and success fees based on the client's budget and the complexity of the transaction. This flexibility made the model more accessible to a wider range of clients and allowed the agent to adapt their services to each client's needs. The agent found that this approach led to more engaged and satisfied clients, as they felt their specific financial situations were considered. The success fee motivated the agent to negotiate the best possible terms for their clients, leading to a high rate of successful transactions and repeat business.

These success stories underscore the potential of the retainer plus success fee model to provide value to clients while ensuring real estate professionals are fairly compensated for their expertise and efforts. By adopting this model, agents can foster transparency, build trust, and tailor their services to meet the diverse needs of their clientele, leading to mutually beneficial outcomes and sustained success in the competitive real estate market.

6. **Custom and A La Carte Services**

   Hourly rates are particularly well-suited for providing custom services not typically included in standard packages. Clients can choose specific tasks they need assistance with, such as drafting lease agreements, consulting on renovation potentials, or developing a property marketing strategy.

7. **Handling Complex Paperwork**

   Clients may seek professional help to navigate the complex paperwork associated with real estate transactions, including contracts, disclosures, and legal documents. Offering these services on an hourly basis allows clients to secure expert assistance without the expense of full-service representation.

Key Considerations

While hourly rates offer flexibility and can align closely with client needs, successful implementation requires clear communication about the scope of services, expected time commitments, and regular updates on hours spent. This transparency builds trust and ensures that clients feel they are receiving value for their investment.

In conclusion, hourly rates in real estate provide a flexible, transparent alternative to traditional commission models, offering benefits in scenarios that require specialized knowledge, targeted support, or custom services. By understanding when hourly rates work best, real estate professionals can tailor their offerings to meet diverse client needs, enhancing satisfaction and fostering long-term relationships.

Sample Retainer Plus Success Fee

Sample

Designing a pricing model that combines a retainer with a success fee requires careful consideration to ensure fairness to both the real estate professional and the client. This model typically involves an upfront retainer fee for initial services and a success fee contingent upon the successful sale or purchase of a property.

Initial Retainer Fee	Success Fee
Retainer Fee: $2,000 - $5,000 This fee covers the initial costs and efforts of the real estate professional, including market analysis, property listing, initial consultations, and marketing efforts. The range accounts for varying market conditions and property types.	**Success Fee Percentage: 1.5% - 3% of the sale/purchase price** The success fee is due upon the successful closing of a real estate transaction. This fee is in addition to the retainer and reflects the agent's success in completing the sale or purchase. The percentage might be lower than traditional commission rates to account for the upfront retainer.

This retainer plus success fee model incentivizes the real estate professional to successfully close transactions while providing clients with a transparent and predictable cost structure. By adjusting the model based on individual circumstances and maintaining open communication, real estate professionals can create a compensation structure that aligns with their clients' interests and the value they provide.

Key Considerations

1. **Adjusting for Retainer:** The success fee should be adjusted to account for the upfront retainer paid by the client. This ensures the total compensation is fair and reflects the value provided throughout the transaction process.
2. **Defining Scope of Services:** Clearly outline what services are included under the retainer fee and what constitutes a successful transaction for the success fee to apply. This clarity prevents misunderstandings and sets clear expectations.
3. **Flexibility:** Be prepared to negotiate the retainer and success fee based on the property's value, complexity of the transaction, and client's needs. Flexibility can help tailor your services to fit your client's unique situation.
4. **Transparent Communication:** Ensure all terms, including how the retainer is applied to the success fee and under what conditions the success fee is earned, are clearly communicated and documented in the contract.

Chapter 5: Subscription Model

The subscription model in real estate is a groundbreaking approach that redefines traditional transaction-based compensation methods, offering continuous, value-driven services for a recurring fee. This innovative model caters to the evolving needs of clients who seek ongoing support, advice, and access to real estate expertise beyond singular transactions. By adopting a subscription-based model, real estate professionals can build longer-term relationships with clients, ensuring a steady stream of income and providing clients with predictable costs for high-quality, personalized services.

Innovating with Real Estate Subscriptions

The subscription model in real estate represents a shift towards a more service-oriented approach, focusing on sustained client engagement and consistent delivery of value over time. This model is particularly suited for clients who require ongoing real estate services, such as investors, developers, or clients interested in periodically adjusting their real estate portfolios.

Key Features of Real Estate Subscriptions:

- ***Regular Access to Expertise***

    Subscribers benefit from regular access to their real estate professional's expertise, receiving personalized advice, market insights, and updates tailored to their specific interests and goals.

- **Flexible Service Offerings**

    Subscription services can range from basic market analysis and investment advice to comprehensive property management, portfolio optimization, and personalized buying or selling strategies.

- **Predictable Costs and Revenue**

    Clients appreciate the predictability of subscription fees, which helps with budgeting for real estate services. For professionals, this model ensures a steady revenue stream, reducing income volatility tied to transaction cycles.

- **Customization and Scalability**

    Subscriptions can be customized to fit various client needs, with different tiers or packages that scale services up or down based on client preferences and changing requirements.

Implementing a Subscription Model:

- **Define Your Offerings**

    Clearly outline the services included at each subscription tier, ensuring there's a distinct value proposition for different client segments.

- **Set Pricing Structures**

    Establish pricing that reflects the value of your offerings while remaining competitive and accessible. Consider factors like market demand, the uniqueness of your services, and the cost of delivering these services continuously.

- **Technology and Infrastructure**

    Invest in the necessary technology and infrastructure to support a subscription model, including client relationship management systems, automated billing platforms, and digital communication tools.

- **Marketing and Client Education**

    Educate potential clients about the benefits of the subscription model through targeted marketing efforts. Highlight the convenience, continuous support, and tailored services that subscribers will enjoy.

- **Feedback and Adaptation**

    Solicit regular feedback from subscribers to refine and adapt your offerings. Being responsive to client needs and market trends will help you maintain relevance and value.

Challenges and Opportunities:

- **Building a Subscriber Base**

    Initially attracting subscribers may be challenging, requiring effective marketing and a clear demonstration of value.

- **Maintaining Service Quality**

    Providing consistent, high-quality services over time is crucial to retaining subscribers and justifying the recurring fee.

The subscription model in real estate offers an exciting avenue for professionals looking to diversify their income streams and deepen client relationships. By focusing on long-term client value and satisfaction, real estate professionals can establish a loyal subscriber base, enhancing both their service impact and business stability in a competitive market.

What Services to Include in Your Subscription

Choosing the right mix of services to include in your real estate subscription model is crucial for delivering value to your clients and ensuring the sustainability of this revenue stream. The services offered should not only cater to the ongoing needs of your clients but also distinguish your subscription from one-time transactional services.

Here are key service categories to consider incorporating into your subscription model:

- **Market Insights and Analysis**
  - Regular Market Reports: Offer in-depth analysis and reports on local real estate market trends, including price movements, inventory levels, and future projections.
  - Investment Opportunities: Highlight potential investment opportunities based on the client's interests and market conditions.

- **Personalized Consultations**
  - Strategy Sessions: Schedule regular strategy sessions to discuss and adjust the client's real estate goals and plans based on changing market conditions or personal circumstances.
  - Portfolio Reviews: Provide periodic reviews of the client's real estate portfolio to suggest optimizations or adjustments.

- **Priority Access to Listings**
  - Early Notifications: Give subscribers early or exclusive access to new listings that match their criteria before they hit the broader market.

- o Off-Market Opportunities: Share insights about off-market or pre-market listings that could offer investment opportunities.

- **Transactional Support**
  - o Negotiation Assistance: Offer negotiation support for buying or selling transactions, ensuring clients get the best possible terms.
  - o Paperwork and Compliance Help: Provide assistance with the complex paperwork and compliance requirements of real estate transactions.

- **Property Management and Maintenance**
  - o Vendor Coordination: Assist with coordinating maintenance or renovation work by connecting clients with trusted vendors and contractors.
  - o Property Monitoring: Offer services such as regular property check-ups or monitoring for clients who own rental properties or second homes.

- **Educational Content and Resources**
  - o Webinars and Workshops: Host exclusive webinars and workshops on various real estate topics, from investment strategies to home improvement tips.
  - o Resource Library: Provide access to a library of resources, including guides, checklists, and templates that can assist clients in managing their real estate activities.

- **Exclusive Perks and Discounts**
  - o Service Discounts: Offer subscribers discounts on additional services or fees.

- Partner Offers: Negotiate deals or discounts with related service providers (home inspectors, legal services, moving companies) exclusively for your subscribers.

Tailoring Your Offerings

- **Customization Based on Client Segments**

    Tailor your subscription tiers or packages to cater to different client segments, such as first-time homebuyers, seasoned investors, or property owners looking for management support.

- **Feedback Loop**

    Establish a feedback mechanism to continuously gather insights from your subscribers about the types of services they find most valuable and any additional services they would like to see offered.

Incorporating a diverse and valuable set of services into your real estate subscription model not only enhances the client experience but also solidifies the client-professional relationship over the long term. By offering a mix of insightful content, personalized advice, and practical support, you can create a subscription model that stands out in the real estate market.

Pricing Strategies for Subscription Services

Developing effective pricing strategies for your real estate subscription services is critical to attracting and retaining clients while ensuring your business remains profitable. The right pricing strategy should reflect the value of the services offered, cater to your target market, and be competitive within the industry.

Here are key considerations for setting your subscription pricing:

- **Cost-Plus Pricing**

    Begin by calculating the total cost of providing your subscription services, including both direct costs (such as software subscriptions, marketing materials, and outsourced services) and indirect costs (like your time and overhead). Add a markup to ensure profitability. This straightforward approach ensures your costs are covered and provides a clear basis for your pricing structure.

- **Value-Based Pricing**

    Value-based pricing focuses on the perceived value of your services to the client rather than the cost of delivering those services. Determine how much your clients are willing to pay by evaluating how your services save them time, money, or stress or by how much they could potentially profit from your advice and assistance. This approach often justifies higher price points because it's directly tied to the benefits received by the client.

- **Tiered Pricing Structure**

    Offering multiple subscription tiers is an effective way to cater to different client needs and budgets. Each tier can offer a progressively more comprehensive package of services, with the price increasing accordingly. This strategy not only accommodates a wider range of clients but also encourages clients to opt for higher tiers to gain access to more valuable services.

    - Basic Tier: Could include market updates, access to an online resource library, and a monthly consultation call.
    - Premium Tier: Might add priority access to new listings, additional monthly consultations, and personalized investment analysis.

- - VIP Tier: Could offer all the above plus exclusive investment opportunities, comprehensive property management services, and unlimited consultations.

- **Competitive Analysis**

  Research the pricing of similar subscription services within the real estate industry and related sectors. Understanding the competitive landscape helps in positioning your subscription attractively in the market. Pricing too high might deter potential clients, while pricing too low could undermine the perceived value of your services.

- **Psychological Pricing**

  Consider psychological pricing strategies that can make your subscription fees more appealing. Pricing a service at $99 instead of $100, for example, can make a significant difference in how the price is perceived by potential clients.

- **Feedback and Flexibility**

  After launching your subscription services, actively seek feedback from your subscribers regarding the pricing and the value they feel they're receiving. Be prepared to adjust your pricing based on this feedback and evolving market conditions to remain competitive and ensure client satisfaction.

- **Transparent Communication**

  Ensure that your pricing structure and what each subscription tier includes are clearly communicated in your marketing materials, on your website, and during consultations with potential clients. Transparency builds trust and helps clients make informed decisions.

Setting the pricing for your real estate subscription services requires a balance between covering your costs, providing value to your clients, and staying competitive in the market. By carefully considering these strategies and being responsive to client feedback and market dynamics, you can establish a successful and profitable subscription model.

Building Long-Term Client Relationships Through Subscriptions

The subscription model in real estate isn't just about providing ongoing services; it's a strategy for cultivating long-term client relationships that can yield benefits for both parties over time. This model encourages continuous engagement, ensuring that clients receive consistent value and support throughout their real estate journey. Here's how real estate professionals can leverage subscriptions to build these enduring connections:

Provide Continuous Value

- **Stay Proactive**

    Regularly offer insights, advice, and updates that keep your clients informed and engaged. Showcasing your ongoing commitment to their real estate success reinforces the value of the subscription.

- **Adapt to Changing Needs**

    Be attentive to shifts in your clients' real estate goals or situations and adjust your services accordingly. Demonstrating flexibility and responsiveness can deepen client trust and loyalty.

Enhance Personal Connection

- **Personalized Service**

    Use the insights gained from ongoing interactions to tailor your services more closely to each client's preferences and needs. Personalization makes clients feel valued and understood, enhancing their satisfaction with your service.

- **Regular Check-ins**

    Schedule periodic check-ins not just to discuss real estate matters but also to strengthen your relationship. These touchpoints can provide valuable feedback and identify new opportunities to assist.

Foster Trust and Reliability

- **Consistency Is Key**

    Ensure that the quality of your services remains high and consistent. Reliability fosters trust, which is the foundation of any long-term relationship.

- **Transparent Communication**

    Keep your clients informed about any changes in your services or pricing and be clear about what they can expect. Transparency eliminates surprises and builds trust.

Create Community

- **Exclusive Events**

    Host events or workshops exclusively for your subscribers. This not only adds value but also fosters a sense of community among your clients, with you at the center.

- **Online Forums or Groups**

    Create an online space where your clients can share experiences, ask questions, and connect with each other. This builds a community around your brand and services.

Reward Loyalty

- **Loyalty Benefits**

    Offer perks or discounts to long-term subscribers as a token of appreciation for their loyalty. This could include discounted services for referrals or special rates on additional services.

- **Feedback and Improvement**

    Actively seek and incorporate client feedback into your services. Showing clients that their opinions matter and can lead to tangible improvements strengthens the relationship.

Building long-term client relationships through subscriptions requires a focus on delivering continuous, personalized value and fostering trust and community. By doing so, real estate professionals can create a loyal client base that not only sustains their business through steady subscription revenue but also amplifies their reputation and reach through referrals and positive word-of-mouth.

Tier Pricing
Sample

Market Insider
$49/month
basic plan

- → Monthly market analysis report
- → Access to online resource library
- → Quarterly investment webinar
- → Newsletter with market updates and tips

Insider Pro
$149/month
premium plan

- → All benefits of the Basic Subscription
- → Bi-weekly personalized market insights email
- → Monthly one-on-one investment strategy session
- → Early access to new listings
- → Discounted rates on transactional services

Portfolio Master
$299/month
vip plan

- → All benefits of the Premium Subscription
- → Unlimited one-on-one consultations
- → Comprehensive annual portfolio review
- → Personalized property management advice
- → Exclusive access to off-market deals
- → Priority support

These prices and services are illustrative and should be adjusted based on your operational costs, the competitive landscape, and the perceived value of your services. Remember, the goal of tiered pricing is not only to cater to different segments of your market but also to encourage clients to opt for higher tiers by clearly demonstrating the additional value they offer. Tailoring the service packages to the specific needs and preferences of your client base can significantly enhance the appeal of your subscription model.

Conclusion

Choosing the Right Model for Your Business

As we conclude our exploration of innovative real estate compensation models, it becomes clear that the choice between traditional commission-based models, flat fee services, hourly rates, retainer plus success fee, and subscription models is not one-size-fits-all. The decision hinges on various factors, including your client base, market dynamics, personal business goals, and the unique value you offer as a real estate professional.

Here's how to approach selecting the right model for your business:

- **Assess Your Market and Clientele**

    Understanding the needs and preferences of your target market is paramount. Are your clients primarily interested in one-off transactions, or do they seek ongoing advice and services? The nature of your clientele will significantly influence which compensation model aligns best with their expectations and your business strategy.

- **Evaluate Your Value Proposition**

    What unique value do you bring to your clients? Are you offering specialized knowledge in a certain type of real estate, exceptional negotiation skills, or perhaps unparalleled market analysis? Identifying your strengths can guide you towards a compensation model that best highlights and monetizes these offerings.

- **Consider Your Business Goals**

    Reflect on your long-term business objectives. Are you aiming for steady, predictable income, or are you more focused on maximizing earnings from high-value transactions? Your business goals can help determine which model provides the financial structure that aligns with your aspirations.

- **Flexibility and Adaptability**

    The real estate market is dynamic, and so are the needs of your clients. Choosing a model that allows for flexibility and adaptability will enable you to adjust your services and pricing as the market evolves, ensuring you remain competitive and responsive.

- **Experimentation and Feedback**

    Don't be afraid to experiment with different models or a hybrid approach to find what works best for you and your clients. Solicit feedback regularly to understand how your chosen model is perceived and where adjustments may be needed to enhance value and satisfaction.

In summary, choosing the right compensation model for your real estate business requires a careful balance of market understanding, self-assessment, and strategic planning. By considering the needs of your clients, the unique value you offer, and your long-term business goals, you can select a model that not only maximizes your earnings but also solidifies your reputation as a trusted, client-focused real estate professional. Embrace flexibility and be prepared to evolve your approach as you gain insights and feedback, ensuring your business model remains both competitive and aligned with your vision for success.

Adapting to Change and Staying Competitive

In the fast-paced world of real estate, adaptation and competitiveness are crucial for sustained success. As market conditions, client expectations, and industry technologies evolve, so too must real estate professionals.

Here's how to stay ahead in a changing landscape:

Embrace Technological Advances

- **Leverage New Tools**

  Stay abreast of the latest real estate technologies, from virtual tour software to CRM systems that enhance client communication. Adopting these tools can improve your efficiency and appeal to tech-savvy clients.

- **Digital Marketing**

  Utilize digital marketing strategies, including social media, SEO, and email marketing, to reach a broader audience and showcase your services effectively.

Continuously Learn and Grow

- **Professional Development**

  Engage in ongoing education and professional development opportunities. Whether through formal education, webinars, or industry conferences, expanding your knowledge base keeps you informed and innovative.

- **Market Analysis**

  Regularly analyze market trends and adapt your strategies accordingly. Understanding shifts in buyer and seller behaviors can help you anticipate needs and adjust your services.

Foster Strong Relationships

- **Client Focus**

    Maintain a strong focus on client relationships. Personalized service and attention to client needs can set you apart in a competitive market.

- **Networking**

    Build and nurture a professional network, including other real estate professionals, lenders, and local businesses. These relationships can provide referrals and insights into market trends.

Diversify Your Services

- **Offer Unique Services**

    Differentiate yourself by offering unique or niche services that meet specific client needs. This could range from specializing in eco-friendly properties to providing extensive relocation services.

- **Flexible Compensation Models**

    Consider offering flexible compensation models, such as the subscription model or retainer plus success fee, to appeal to a wider range of clients.

Stay Client-Centric

- **Feedback Loop**

    Create a system for regularly gathering and acting on client feedback. Understanding your clients' experiences and needs can guide your service enhancements and innovations.

- **Adapt to Client Needs**

    Be prepared to adapt your services and communication styles to meet the changing needs of your clients. This flexibility can make you a preferred choice for clients with diverse needs.

Evaluate and Iterate

- **Regular Business Reviews**

    Conduct regular reviews of your business strategies, financial performance, and client satisfaction metrics. This introspection can reveal areas for improvement or expansion.

- **Be Open to Change**

    The willingness to pivot your business model or strategy in response to feedback, market changes, or new opportunities is essential for staying competitive.

Adapting to change and staying competitive in the real estate industry requires a proactive approach to technology, education, client relationships, and service offerings. By embracing innovation, prioritizing client needs, and continuously seeking growth opportunities, real estate professionals can navigate the complexities of the market and thrive in an ever-evolving landscape.

The Future of Real Estate Compensation

The future of real estate compensation is poised for innovation, driven by evolving technology, changing consumer expectations, and the increasing demand for transparency and flexibility in the industry. As we look ahead, several key trends are likely to shape how real estate professionals are compensated:

Increased Customization and Client Choice

The trend toward more customized compensation models, including flat fees, subscription services, and hybrid models like retainer plus success fee, is expected to continue. These models offer clients more choice and flexibility, allowing them to select the services and payment structures that best meet their needs. This shift reflects a broader move towards a more client-centered approach in the real estate industry.

Technology-Enabled Services

Advancements in technology will further influence compensation models by enabling new services and efficiencies. For example, the use of big data and AI can offer more personalized market insights and predictions, adding value to subscription services. Blockchain technology might streamline transactions and reduce costs, impacting how transaction-based fees are structured. As real estate professionals incorporate these technologies into their services, compensation models will need to adapt to reflect these added values and efficiencies.

Emphasis on Transparency

There's a growing demand for transparency in all aspects of real estate transactions, including compensation. Clients want to understand exactly what services they are paying for and how much they cost. This push for transparency will likely lead to more detailed breakdowns of services and costs, making it easier for clients to compare options and make informed decisions.

Collaborative and Performance-Based Models

There's potential for more collaborative and performance-based compensation models that align the interests of real estate professionals and their clients more closely. Models that reward agents for exceeding client expectations, achieving better sale prices, or securing properties under budget can incentivize higher performance and foster stronger client-agent relationships.

Regulatory Influences

Regulatory changes could also impact compensation models in the real estate industry. As governments and regulatory bodies look to increase transparency and fairness in real estate transactions, they may introduce guidelines or restrictions on how agents can be compensated. Staying informed and compliant with these regulations will be crucial for real estate professionals.

Sustainable Business Practices

Finally, the rise of social and environmental consciousness among consumers may lead to compensation models that reward sustainable business practices. Real estate professionals who specialize in eco-friendly properties or who demonstrate a commitment to social responsibility may be able to command higher fees or attract more clients through unique compensation models that reflect these values.

The future of real estate compensation is dynamic and will likely see continued innovation and change. Real estate professionals who are adaptable, client-focused, and technologically savvy will be well-positioned to navigate these changes and thrive in the evolving market landscape.

Appendices

Glossary of Terms

Commission-Based Model:

A traditional compensation structure where real estate professionals earn a percentage of the sale price of a property.

Flat Fee Services:

A compensation model where real estate agents charge a predetermined, fixed amount for their services, regardless of the property's sale price.

Hourly Rates:

A payment model where agents are compensated based on the actual time they spend working on a client's transaction.

Fee-for-Service (FFS):

A flexible pricing structure where clients pay individually for each discrete service provided by the real estate professional.

Retainer Fee:

An upfront fee paid by the client to secure the services of a real estate professional, often used in conjunction with a success fee in hybrid compensation models.

Success Fee:

A fee that is contingent upon the successful conclusion of a real estate transaction, typically used in hybrid models together with a retainer fee.

Subscription Model:

A modern compensation model in real estate where clients pay a recurring fee for ongoing access to a suite of services.

MLS (Multiple Listing Service):

A database established by cooperating real estate brokers to provide data about properties for sale.

NAR (National Association of Realtors):

A major American trade association for real estate professionals, involved in all aspects of the residential and commercial real estate industries.

Regulatory Compliance:

Adhering to laws and regulations in the real estate industry, which can vary by location and affect compensation practices and other aspects of real estate transactions.

Market Analysis:

The evaluation of the real estate market to understand trends, pricing, and the supply and demand dynamics relevant to property transactions.

Portfolio Management:

The art of managing a client's collection of real estate investments to maximize profitability and align with investment goals.

Real Estate Transaction Management:

The process of managing all the components of a real estate transaction from initial contract to closing, ensuring all parties meet their obligations efficiently.

Negotiation Assistance:

Support provided by real estate professionals to help clients negotiate terms of sale or purchase that are favorable.

Client Empowerment:

Strategies and practices that enhance the client's control over the real estate transaction process, typically through education and flexible service options.

Closing Costs:

Fees and expenses, over and above the price of the property, incurred by buyers and sellers in transferring ownership of a property.

Listing Agent:

A real estate professional who represents the seller in a property transaction, responsible for listing the property and facilitating its sale.

Buyer's Agent:

A real estate professional who represents the buyer in a property transaction, helping the buyer find and purchase a property.

Exclusive Listing:

A contract under which the listing broker acts as the agent or as the legally recognized non-agency representative of the seller(s), and the seller(s) agrees to pay a commission to the listing broker regardless of whether the property is sold through the efforts of the listing broker, the seller, or anyone else.

Open House:

A scheduled period of time in which a house or other dwelling is designated to be open for viewing by potential buyers.

Real Estate Broker:

A person or company licensed to negotiate and arrange real estate sales; can work as an agent for a buyer or seller.

Property Valuation:

The process of determining the economic value of a real estate investment, typically conducted by a professional appraiser.

Market Dynamics:

The forces that impact the supply and demand of properties in the real estate market, influencing pricing and availability.

Transactional Services:

Services provided by real estate professionals that are related to the buying or selling of a property, including contract negotiation, documentation, and closing services.

Real Estate Portfolio:

A collection of real estate investments owned by an individual, a group, or a company, including various property types such as residential, commercial, and land investments.

Legal Compliance:

Adherence to laws and regulations governing real estate transactions, including those related to disclosures, contracts, and agency relationships.

Client Consultation:

Meetings or discussions between a real estate professional and a client to understand the client's needs, preferences, and financial objectives in order to provide tailored advice.

Vendor Coordination:

The process of managing relationships and engagements with third-party service providers during the real estate transaction process, such as home inspectors, appraisers, and contractors.

Capital Gains:

The profit made from the sale of real estate or investments, which may be subject to capital gains tax depending on the amount of time the property was held and other factors.

Escrow:

A financial arrangement where a third party holds and regulates payment of the funds required for two parties involved in a given transaction, helping make transactions safer by keeping the payment in a secure escrow account which is only released when all of the terms of an agreement are met as overseen by the escrow company.

Additional Resources

Books:

"The Millionaire Real Estate Agent" by Gary Keller

Offers insights into the strategies used by successful real estate agents.

"Your First Year in Real Estate" by Dirk Zeller

A beginner's guide to navigating the challenges and opportunities in real estate.

"Real Estate Market Analysis: Methods and Case Studies" by Deborah L. Brett

Provides a thorough overview of performing market analyses.

Websites:

Realtor.com

Offers a comprehensive look at market trends, property listings, and educational content for both buyers and agents.

Zillow Research

A source for housing data, economic trends, and insights into both local and national real estate markets.

National Association of Realtors (NAR)

Provides a wide range of statistics, studies, and reports about the real estate industry.

Tools:

MLS.com

Multiple Listing Service that provides information about properties for sale and real estate market data.

Real Estate Analysis Software, such as ARGUS or CoStar

Advanced tools for real estate market analysis, investment analysis, and portfolio management.

BiggerPockets Real Estate Investment Calculator

Tools for analyzing rental properties, house flips, and wholesaling deals for profitability.

Industry Reports:

Annual Real Estate Market Reports by JLL

Provides detailed analysis and forecasts for various real estate sectors globally.

CBRE Research Gateway

Offers comprehensive research on commercial real estate trends around the world.

Emerging Trends in Real Estate by Urban Land Institute and PwC

An annual report detailing the trends and outlook in real estate investment and development.

Online Courses and Webinars:

"Introduction to Commercial Real Estate Analysis" on Lynda/LinkedIn Learning

Offers foundational knowledge and skills for new real estate professionals.

"Real Estate Financial Modeling Bootcamp" on Udemy

Provides detailed instruction on financial modeling for real estate investments.

"Certified Commercial Advisor (CCA) Certification" by the National Association of Commercial Real Estate Advisors

A comprehensive certification program for those focusing on commercial real estate.

Podcasts:

"The BiggerPockets Real Estate Podcast"

Features interviews with real estate investors and professionals offering actionable advice.

"Real Estate Coaching Radio" by Tim and Julie Harris

Provides coaching and updated news on real estate strategies and market conditions.

FAQs on Transitioning to New Compensation Structures

Q1: How will the new compensation structures impact my earnings as a real estate agent?

A: The impact on earnings will vary based on the compensation model you choose, your market area, and how you adapt your services to meet client needs. Flexibility in your service offerings and transparency in pricing can help maintain or even increase your earnings.

Q2: Can I still receive a commission under the new models?

A: Yes, commissions are still possible, particularly under the retainer plus success fee and subscription models. These models may offer more predictability in income and align closely with providing ongoing value to clients.

Q3: How do I explain these changes to my clients?

A: Clear communication and education are key. Explain the benefits of the new model you're adopting, such as increased transparency, potentially lower costs, and services tailored to their specific needs. Providing examples and scenarios can also help illustrate the advantages.

Q4: Will I need to adjust my marketing strategies with these new models?

A: Yes, adapting your marketing strategies to highlight the unique benefits of your chosen compensation model is essential. This might include emphasizing the transparency of flat fee services, the personalized and ongoing support of subscription services, or the aligned incentives of a retainer plus success fee model.

Q5: How should I structure my contracts under these new models?

A: Contracts should clearly outline the services provided, the compensation structure, and any terms and conditions specific to the model you're using. It's advisable to consult with a legal professional to ensure your contracts are comprehensive and compliant with local regulations.

Q6: What if a client prefers the traditional commission model?

A: While transitioning to new models, it's important to maintain flexibility and accommodate clients who prefer traditional methods. Explaining the benefits of new models while offering options can help clients make informed decisions that suit their preferences.

Q7: How can I ensure I'm competitively priced under these new models?

A: Conduct market research to understand the pricing landscape for similar services in your area. Consider the value you provide, your experience, and the specific needs of your target clientele when setting your prices.

Q8: Are these new compensation models compliant with real estate regulations?

A: Most new compensation models are designed to be compliant with regulations, emphasizing transparency and client choice. However, staying informed about local laws and consulting with legal advisors is crucial to ensure compliance.

Transitioning to new compensation structures represents a significant shift in the real estate industry, aimed at offering more transparency, flexibility, and value to clients.

Embracing these changes requires adaptation and a client-centered approach, but it also opens up opportunities for innovation and growth in your real estate practice.

Real Estate Services Agreement (Flat Fee)

This Agreement is made on [Date], between [Real Estate Professional Name], hereinafter referred to as "Agent," and [Client Name], hereinafter referred to as "Client."

1. Services Provided: The Agent agrees to provide the Client with the following real estate services for a flat fee:
    - Listing the property on the Multiple Listing Service (MLS)
    - Professional photography for listing purposes
    - Marketing the property through various channels
    - Conducting open houses
    - Negotiation support with potential buyers
    - Assistance with closing documentation

2. Flat Fee: The Client agrees to pay the Agent a flat fee of [Amount] for the services outlined above. This fee is due upon signing this Agreement and is non-refundable.

3. Term: This Agreement shall commence on [Start Date] and conclude upon the successful sale of the property or on [End Date], whichever occurs first.

4. Responsibilities of the Client: The Client agrees to:
    - Provide the Agent with all necessary access and information required to perform the services.
    - Make the property available for showings and open houses as agreed upon with the Agent.
    - Review and approve marketing materials in a timely manner.

5. Confidentiality: Both parties agree to keep all information related to the property and the transaction confidential, except as required by law or necessary to perform the services.

6. Dispute Resolution: Any disputes arising from this Agreement shall be resolved through mediation, if possible. If mediation is unsuccessful, disputes shall be settled through binding arbitration.

7. Entire Agreement: This Agreement constitutes the entire agreement between the Agent and the Client, superseding all prior agreements and understandings, whether written or oral.

8. Governing Law: This Agreement shall be governed by the laws of [State/Country].

Signatures:

Agent's Signature: _____ Date: _____

Client's Signature: _____ Date: _____

This template is a starting point and can be customized based on specific services offered, local regulations, and individual client needs. Always have a legal professional review your contracts to ensure they are comprehensive, compliant, and correctly reflect the agreement between you and your client.

Real Estate Services Agreement (Hourly Rate)

This Agreement is made on [Date], between [Real Estate Professional Name], hereinafter referred to as "Agent," and [Client Name], hereinafter referred to as "Client."

1. Scope of Services: The Agent agrees to provide the Client with real estate services on an hourly basis, including but not limited to:
    - Property search and showings
    - Market analysis
    - Negotiation of purchase or lease agreements
    - Documentation and closing support
    - Consultation services

2. Hourly Rate: The Client agrees to compensate the Agent at an hourly rate of [Amount] for all services rendered under this Agreement.

3. Billing and Payment:
    - The Agent will provide the Client with an itemized invoice detailing hours worked and services rendered on a [weekly/monthly] basis.
    - Payment is due within [number] days of invoice receipt.
    - Any late payments will incur a late fee of [percentage] per month on the outstanding balance.

4. Term: This Agreement will commence on [Start Date] and continue until terminated by either party with [number] days written notice. Services may be concluded earlier upon the completion of the Client's real estate transaction.

5. Client Responsibilities: The Client agrees to:
    - Provide timely information and access as needed for the Agent to perform services.
    - Make decisions and approvals promptly to avoid delays in the real estate process.

6. Confidentiality: Both parties agree to maintain the confidentiality of all proprietary information, except as required by law or necessary for the performance of the services.

7. Independent Contractor Status: The Agent is engaged as an independent contractor, not an employee of the Client.

8. Dispute Resolution: In the event of a dispute, both parties will seek resolution through good faith negotiation. If unresolved, disputes shall be subject to arbitration in accordance with the rules of [Arbitration Association].

9. Governing Law: This Agreement shall be governed by the laws of [State/Country].

10. Entire Agreement: This document and any attached exhibits constitute the entire agreement between the parties, superseding all prior agreements and understandings, whether oral or written.

Signatures:

Agent's Signature: _____ Date: _____

Client's Signature: _____ Date: _____

This template is a starting point and can be customized based on specific services offered, local regulations, and individual client needs. Always have a legal professional review your contracts to ensure they are comprehensive, compliant, and correctly reflect the agreement between you and your client.

Real Estate Services Agreement (Fee for Service)

This Agreement is made on [Date], between [Real Estate Professional Name], hereinafter referred to as "Agent," and [Client Name], hereinafter referred to as "Client."

1. Services Provided: The Agent agrees to provide the Client with real estate services as detailed in Attachment A (Service Menu and Pricing), incorporated herein by reference. Such services may include, but are not limited to, listing the property, conducting market analysis, providing purchase assistance, and facilitating closing procedures.

2. Fee Structure: The Client agrees to pay the Agent a fee for service as outlined in Attachment A. Each service provided by the Agent to the Client shall be billed according to the agreed-upon fee structure.

3. Payment Terms:
    - Payment for each service is due upon completion of the said service to the satisfaction of the Client.
    - The Agent will provide an itemized invoice detailing the services rendered and the associated fees.

4. Term and Termination: This Agreement shall commence on [Start Date] and shall continue until either party terminates the Agreement with [Number] days written notice, or all services under the Agreement are completed and paid.

5. Responsibilities of the Client: The Client agrees to:
    - Provide all necessary information and access required by the Agent to perform the services.
    - Make timely decisions and approvals to facilitate the completion of services.

6. Confidentiality: Both the Agent and the Client agree to maintain the confidentiality of all information related to the property, transaction, and services provided.

7. Independent Contractor: It is understood that the Agent is acting as an independent contractor and not as an employee of the Client.

8. Governing Law: This Agreement shall be governed by the laws of [State/Country].

9. Entire Agreement: This Agreement, including Attachment A, constitutes the entire agreement between the parties and supersedes all prior understandings, agreements, and representations.

10. Amendments: Any amendments to this Agreement must be in writing and signed by both parties.

Signatures:

Agent's Signature: _____ Date: _____

Client's Signature: _____ Date: _____

This template is a starting point and can be customized based on specific services offered, local regulations, and individual client needs. Always have a legal professional review your contracts to ensure they are comprehensive, compliant, and correctly reflect the agreement between you and your client.

Real Estate Services Agreement
(Retainer Plus Success Fee Real Estate Agreement)

This Agreement is made on [Date], between [Real Estate Professional Name], hereinafter referred to as "Agent," and [Client Name], hereinafter referred to as "Client."

1. Services: The Agent agrees to provide comprehensive real estate services aimed at the sale/purchase of the property listed at [Property Address], including but not limited to market analysis, listing services, marketing, negotiations, and transaction management.

2. Retainer Fee:
   - The Client agrees to pay the Agent a non-refundable retainer fee of [Retainer Fee Amount] upon the execution of this Agreement.
   - The retainer fee covers initial consultations, property evaluation, listing preparation, and marketing efforts.

3. Success Fee:
   - Upon the successful closing of a sale or purchase transaction of the property, the Client agrees to pay the Agent a success fee.
   - The success fee will be [Percentage]% of the final sale or purchase price.
   - The retainer fee previously paid shall be credited against the success fee due at closing.

4. Term: This Agreement shall commence on the date signed and shall continue until the completion of the sale/purchase transaction or until terminated by either party with [Notice Period] days' notice.

5. Obligations of the Client: The Client shall cooperate with the Agent by providing necessary information, making the property available for showings, and making timely decisions as required.

6. Confidentiality: Both parties agree to maintain the confidentiality of all proprietary information related to the transaction and services provided.

7. Independent Contractor Status: It is agreed that the Agent is acting as an independent contractor and not as an employee of the Client.

8. Dispute Resolution: Any disputes arising from this Agreement shall first attempt to be resolved through mediation. If unsuccessful, arbitration shall be pursued as the next course of action.

9. Governing Law: This Agreement shall be governed by the laws of [State/Country].

10. Entire Agreement: This document and any attached exhibits constitute the entire agreement between the Agent and the Client regarding the subject matter hereof.

Signatures:

Agent's Signature: _____ Date: _____
Client's Signature: _____ Date: _____

This template is a starting point and can be customized based on specific services offered, local regulations, and individual client needs. Always have a legal professional review your contracts to ensure they are comprehensive, compliant, and correctly reflect the agreement between you and your client.

Real Estate Services Agreement (Subscription Model)

This Agreement is made on [Date], between [Real Estate Professional Name], hereinafter referred to as "Agent," and [Client Name], hereinafter referred to as "Client."

1. Subscription Services: The Agent agrees to provide the Client with ongoing real estate services, including but not limited to market updates, property listings, investment advice, and personal consultations as part of a subscription plan.

2. Subscription Fee:
   - The Client agrees to pay a recurring subscription fee of [Subscription Fee Amount] per [month/year].
   - The first payment is due upon signing this Agreement, with subsequent payments due on the [day] of each [month/year].

3. Term and Cancellation:
   - This subscription is effective from [Start Date] and shall continue on a rolling basis until canceled by either party.
   - Either party may cancel the subscription with [Notice Period] days' written notice to the other party.

4. Services Included: The specific services included in the subscription are detailed in Attachment A (Service Description), which may include access to exclusive listings, regular consultations, and personalized market analyses.

5. Additional Services: Services not included within the standard subscription may be available for an additional fee, as agreed upon by both parties.

6. Confidentiality: Both parties agree to maintain the confidentiality of all information related to the services provided and the Client's real estate interests.

7. Independent Contractor Status: The Agent is engaged as an independent contractor and not as an employee of the Client.

8. Dispute Resolution: Any disputes arising under this Agreement shall be resolved through mediation or, failing that, by binding arbitration in accordance with the rules of [Arbitration Association].

9. Governing Law: This Agreement shall be governed by the laws of [State/Country].

10. Entire Agreement: This Agreement, including Attachment A, represents the entire agreement between the Agent and the Client concerning the subject matter herein and supersedes all prior agreements and understandings.

Signatures:

Agent's Signature: _____ Date: _____

Client's Signature: _____ Date: _____

This template is a starting point and can be customized based on specific services offered, local regulations, and individual client needs. Always have a legal professional review your contracts to ensure they are comprehensive, compliant, and correctly reflect the agreement between you and your client.

www.ingramcontent.com/pod-product-compliance
Lightning Source LLC
Chambersburg PA
CBHW071212240526
45470CB00018B/1808